# Password Log

**Name:** _____

**Phone:** _____

**Email:** _____

**Company:** _____

**Street:** _____

**City, State, Zip:** _____

## A

| Website URL: |
| --- |
| Username: |
| Email: |
| Password(s): |
| |
| |
| Security Question/Notes |
| |
| |

## A

| Website URL: |
| --- |
| Username: |
| Email: |
| Password(s): |
| |
| |
| Security Question/Notes |
| |
| |

## A

| Website URL: |
| --- |
| Username: |
| Email: |
| Password(s): |
| |
| |
| Security Question/Notes |
| |
| |

## A

| | |
|---|---|
| **Website URL:** | |
| **Username:** | |
| **Email:** | |
| **Password(s):** | |
| | |
| | |
| **Security Question/Notes** | |
| | |
| | |

## A

| | |
|---|---|
| **Website URL:** | |
| **Username:** | |
| **Email:** | |
| **Password(s):** | |
| | |
| | |
| **Security Question/Notes** | |
| | |
| | |

## A

| | |
|---|---|
| **Website URL:** | |
| **Username:** | |
| **Email:** | |
| **Password(s):** | |
| | |
| | |
| **Security Question/Notes** | |
| | |
| | |

## A

| Website URL: | |
|---|---|
| Username: | |
| Email: | |
| Password(s): | |
| | |
| | |
| Security Question/Notes | |
| | |
| | |

## A

| Website URL: | |
|---|---|
| Username: | |
| Email: | |
| Password(s): | |
| | |
| | |
| Security Question/Notes | |
| | |
| | |

## A

| Website URL: | |
|---|---|
| Username: | |
| Email: | |
| Password(s): | |
| | |
| | |
| Security Question/Notes | |
| | |
| | |

## A

| | |
|---|---|
| **Website URL:** | |
| **Username:** | |
| **Email:** | |
| **Password(s):** | |
| | |
| | |
| **Security Question/Notes** | |
| | |
| | |

## A

| | |
|---|---|
| **Website URL:** | |
| **Username:** | |
| **Email:** | |
| **Password(s):** | |
| | |
| | |
| **Security Question/Notes** | |
| | |
| | |

## A

| | |
|---|---|
| **Website URL:** | |
| **Username:** | |
| **Email:** | |
| **Password(s):** | |
| | |
| | |
| **Security Question/Notes** | |
| | |
| | |

**B**

| Website URL: |
| --- |
| Username: |
| Email: |
| Password(s): |
| |
| |
| **Security Question/Notes** |
| |
| |

**B**

| Website URL: |
| --- |
| Username: |
| Email: |
| Password(s): |
| |
| |
| **Security Question/Notes** |
| |
| |

**B**

| Website URL: |
| --- |
| Username: |
| Email: |
| Password(s): |
| |
| |
| **Security Question/Notes** |
| |
| |

**B**

| Website URL: |
| --- |
| Username: |
| Email: |
| Password(s): |
| |
| |
| Security Question/Notes |
| |
| |

**B**

| Website URL: |
| --- |
| Username: |
| Email: |
| Password(s): |
| |
| |
| Security Question/Notes |
| |
| |

**B**

| Website URL: |
| --- |
| Username: |
| Email: |
| Password(s): |
| |
| |
| Security Question/Notes |
| |
| |

## B

**Website URL:**

**Username:**

**Email:**

**Password(s):**

**Security Question/Notes**

## B

**Website URL:**

**Username:**

**Email:**

**Password(s):**

**Security Question/Notes**

## B

**Website URL:**

**Username:**

**Email:**

**Password(s):**

**Security Question/Notes**

**B**

| Website URL: |
| --- |
| Username: |
| Email: |
| Password(s): |
| |
| |
| Security Question/Notes |
| |
| |

**B**

| Website URL: |
| --- |
| Username: |
| Email: |
| Password(s): |
| |
| |
| Security Question/Notes |
| |
| |

**B**

| Website URL: |
| --- |
| Username: |
| Email: |
| Password(s): |
| |
| |
| Security Question/Notes |
| |
| |

## C

| | |
|---|---|
| **Website URL:** | |
| **Username:** | |
| **Email:** | |
| **Password(s):** | |
| | |
| | |
| **Security Question/Notes** | |
| | |
| | |

## C

| | |
|---|---|
| **Website URL:** | |
| **Username:** | |
| **Email:** | |
| **Password(s):** | |
| | |
| | |
| **Security Question/Notes** | |
| | |
| | |

## C

| | |
|---|---|
| **Website URL:** | |
| **Username:** | |
| **Email:** | |
| **Password(s):** | |
| | |
| | |
| **Security Question/Notes** | |
| | |
| | |

## C

| | |
|---|---|
| **Website URL:** | |
| **Username:** | |
| **Email:** | |
| **Password(s):** | |
| | |
| | |
| **Security Question/Notes** | |
| | |
| | |

## C

| | |
|---|---|
| **Website URL:** | |
| **Username:** | |
| **Email:** | |
| **Password(s):** | |
| | |
| | |
| **Security Question/Notes** | |
| | |
| | |

## C

| | |
|---|---|
| **Website URL:** | |
| **Username:** | |
| **Email:** | |
| **Password(s):** | |
| | |
| | |
| **Security Question/Notes** | |
| | |
| | |

## C

| | |
|---|---|
| **Website URL:** | |
| **Username:** | |
| **Email:** | |
| **Password(s):** | |
| | |
| | |
| **Security Question/Notes** | |
| | |
| | |

## C

| | |
|---|---|
| **Website URL:** | |
| **Username:** | |
| **Email:** | |
| **Password(s):** | |
| | |
| | |
| **Security Question/Notes** | |
| | |
| | |

## C

| | |
|---|---|
| **Website URL:** | |
| **Username:** | |
| **Email:** | |
| **Password(s):** | |
| | |
| | |
| **Security Question/Notes** | |
| | |
| | |

## C

| Website URL: |
| --- |
| Username: |
| Email: |
| Password(s): |
| |
| |
| Security Question/Notes |
| |
| |

## C

| Website URL: |
| --- |
| Username: |
| Email: |
| Password(s): |
| |
| |
| Security Question/Notes |
| |
| |

## C

| Website URL: |
| --- |
| Username: |
| Email: |
| Password(s): |
| |
| |
| Security Question/Notes |
| |
| |

**D**

| Website URL: |
|---|
| Username: |
| Email: |
| Password(s): |
| |
| |
| **Security Question/Notes** |
| |
| |

**D**

| Website URL: |
|---|
| Username: |
| Email: |
| Password(s): |
| |
| |
| **Security Question/Notes** |
| |
| |

**D**

| Website URL: |
|---|
| Username: |
| Email: |
| Password(s): |
| |
| |
| **Security Question/Notes** |
| |
| |

**D**

| Website URL: |
| --- |
| Username: |
| Email: |
| Password(s): |
| |
| |
| **Security Question/Notes** |
| |
| |

**D**

| Website URL: |
| --- |
| Username: |
| Email: |
| Password(s): |
| |
| |
| **Security Question/Notes** |
| |
| |

**D**

| Website URL: |
| --- |
| Username: |
| Email: |
| Password(s): |
| |
| |
| **Security Question/Notes** |
| |
| |

**D**

Website URL:

Username:

Email:

Password(s):



Security Question/Notes




**D**

Website URL:

Username:

Email:

Password(s):



Security Question/Notes




**D**

Website URL:

Username:

Email:

Password(s):



Security Question/Notes

**D**

| Website URL: |
| --- |
| Username: |
| Email: |
| Password(s): |
| |
| |
| Security Question/Notes |
| |
| |

**D**

| Website URL: |
| --- |
| Username: |
| Email: |
| Password(s): |
| |
| |
| Security Question/Notes |
| |
| |

**D**

| Website URL: |
| --- |
| Username: |
| Email: |
| Password(s): |
| |
| |
| Security Question/Notes |
| |
| |

**E**

| Website URL: |
| --- |
| Username: |
| Email: |
| Password(s): |
| |
| |
| Security Question/Notes |
| |
| |

**E**

| Website URL: |
| --- |
| Username: |
| Email: |
| Password(s): |
| |
| |
| Security Question/Notes |
| |
| |

**E**

| Website URL: |
| --- |
| Username: |
| Email: |
| Password(s): |
| |
| |
| Security Question/Notes |
| |
| |

**E**

| | |
|---|---|
| **Website URL:** | |
| **Username:** | |
| **Email:** | |
| **Password(s):** | |
| | |
| | |
| **Security Question/Notes** | |
| | |
| | |

**E**

| | |
|---|---|
| **E** | |
| **Username:** | |
| **Email:** | |
| **Password(s):** | |
| | |
| | |
| **Security Question/Notes** | |
| | |
| | |

**E**

| | |
|---|---|
| **Website URL:** | |
| **Username:** | |
| **Email:** | |
| **Password(s):** | |
| | |
| | |
| **Security Question/Notes** | |
| | |
| | |

## E

Website URL:

Username:

Email:

Password(s):

 

 

Security Question/Notes

 

 

## E

Website URL:

Username:

Email:

Password(s):

 

 

Security Question/Notes

 

 

## E

Website URL:

Username:

Email:

Password(s):

 

 

Security Question/Notes

 

 

## E

| | |
|---|---|
| **Website URL:** | |
| **Username:** | |
| **Email:** | |
| **Password(s):** | |
| | |
| | |
| **Security Question/Notes** | |
| | |
| | |

## E

| | |
|---|---|
| **Website URL:** | |
| **Username:** | |
| **Email:** | |
| **Password(s):** | |
| | |
| | |
| **Security Question/Notes** | |
| | |
| | |

## E

| | |
|---|---|
| **Website URL:** | |
| **Username:** | |
| **Email:** | |
| **Password(s):** | |
| | |
| | |
| **Security Question/Notes** | |
| | |
| | |

**F**

| Website URL: |
| --- |
| Username: |
| Email: |
| Password(s): |
| |
| |
| **Security Question/Notes** |
| |
| |

**F**

| Website URL: |
| --- |
| Username: |
| Email: |
| Password(s): |
| |
| |
| **Security Question/Notes** |
| |
| |

**F**

| Website URL: |
| --- |
| Username: |
| Email: |
| Password(s): |
| |
| |
| **Security Question/Notes** |
| |
| |

**F**

| | |
|---|---|
| **Website URL:** | |
| **Username:** | |
| **Email:** | |
| **Password(s):** | |
| | |
| | |
| **Security Question/Notes** | |
| | |
| | |

**F**

| | |
|---|---|
| **Website URL:** | |
| **Username:** | |
| **Email:** | |
| **Password(s):** | |
| | |
| | |
| **Security Question/Notes** | |
| | |
| | |

**F**

| | |
|---|---|
| **Website URL:** | |
| **Username:** | |
| **Email:** | |
| **Password(s):** | |
| | |
| | |
| **Security Question/Notes** | |
| | |
| | |

**F**

| | |
|---|---|
| **Website URL:** | |
| **Username:** | |
| **Email:** | |
| **Password(s):** | |
| | |
| | |
| **Security Question/Notes** | |
| | |
| | |

**F**

| | |
|---|---|
| **Website URL:** | |
| **Username:** | |
| **Email:** | |
| **Password(s):** | |
| | |
| | |
| **Security Question/Notes** | |
| | |
| | |

**F**

| | |
|---|---|
| **Website URL:** | |
| **Username:** | |
| **Email:** | |
| **Password(s):** | |
| | |
| | |
| **Security Question/Notes** | |
| | |
| | |

**F**

| Website URL: |
|---|
| Username: |
| Email: |
| Password(s): |
| |
| |
| Security Question/Notes |
| |
| |

**F**

| Website URL: |
|---|
| Username: |
| Email: |
| Password(s): |
| |
| |
| Security Question/Notes |
| |
| |

**F**

| Website URL: |
|---|
| Username: |
| Email: |
| Password(s): |
| |
| |
| Security Question/Notes |
| |
| |

## G

| | |
|---|---|
| **Website URL:** | |
| **Username:** | |
| **Email:** | |
| **Password(s):** | |
| | |
| | |
| **Security Question/Notes** | |
| | |
| | |

## G

| | |
|---|---|
| **Website URL:** | |
| **Username:** | |
| **Email:** | |
| **Password(s):** | |
| | |
| | |
| **Security Question/Notes** | |
| | |
| | |

## G

| | |
|---|---|
| **Website URL:** | |
| **Username:** | |
| **Email:** | |
| **Password(s):** | |
| | |
| | |
| **Security Question/Notes** | |
| | |
| | |

**G**

| Website URL: |
| --- |
| Username: |
| Email: |
| Password(s): |
| |
| |
| Security Question/Notes |
| |
| |

**G**

| Website URL: |
| --- |
| Username: |
| Email: |
| Password(s): |
| |
| |
| Security Question/Notes |
| |
| |

**G**

| Website URL: |
| --- |
| Username: |
| Email: |
| Password(s): |
| |
| |
| Security Question/Notes |
| |
| |

## G

**Website URL:**

**Username:**

**Email:**

**Password(s):**

**Security Question/Notes**

## G

**Website URL:**

**Username:**

**Email:**

**Password(s):**

**Security Question/Notes**

## G

**Website URL:**

**Username:**

**Email:**

**Password(s):**

**Security Question/Notes**

**G**

| Website URL: |
|---|
| Username: |
| Email: |
| Password(s): |
| |
| |
| **Security Question/Notes** |
| |
| |

**G**

| Website URL: |
|---|
| Username: |
| Email: |
| Password(s): |
| |
| |
| **Security Question/Notes** |
| |
| |

**G**

| Website URL: |
|---|
| Username: |
| Email: |
| Password(s): |
| |
| |
| **Security Question/Notes** |
| |
| |

## H

| Website URL: |
|---|
| Username: |
| Email: |
| Password(s): |
| |
| |
| **Security Question/Notes** |
| |
| |

## H

| Website URL: |
|---|
| Username: |
| Email: |
| Password(s): |
| |
| |
| **Security Question/Notes** |
| |
| |

## H

| Website URL: |
|---|
| Username: |
| Email: |
| Password(s): |
| |
| |
| **Security Question/Notes** |
| |
| |

## H

| | |
|---|---|
| **Website URL:** | |
| **Username:** | |
| **Email:** | |
| **Password(s):** | |
| | |
| | |
| **Security Question/Notes** | |
| | |
| | |

## H

| | |
|---|---|
| **Website URL:** | |
| **Username:** | |
| **Email:** | |
| **Password(s):** | |
| | |
| | |
| **Security Question/Notes** | |
| | |
| | |

## H

| | |
|---|---|
| **Website URL:** | |
| **Username:** | |
| **Email:** | |
| **Password(s):** | |
| | |
| | |
| **Security Question/Notes** | |
| | |
| | |

## H

| | |
|---|---|
| **Website URL:** | |
| **Username:** | |
| **Email:** | |
| **Password(s):** | |
| | |
| | |
| **Security Question/Notes** | |
| | |
| | |

## H

| | |
|---|---|
| **Website URL:** | |
| **Username:** | |
| **Email:** | |
| **Password(s):** | |
| | |
| | |
| **Security Question/Notes** | |
| | |
| | |

## H

| | |
|---|---|
| **Website URL:** | |
| **Username:** | |
| **Email:** | |
| **Password(s):** | |
| | |
| | |
| **Security Question/Notes** | |
| | |
| | |

## H

| | |
|---|---|
| **Website URL:** | |
| **Username:** | |
| **Email:** | |
| **Password(s):** | |
| | |
| | |
| **Security Question/Notes** | |
| | |
| | |

## H

| | |
|---|---|
| **Website URL:** | |
| **Username:** | |
| **Email:** | |
| **Password(s):** | |
| | |
| | |
| **Security Question/Notes** | |
| | |
| | |

## H

| | |
|---|---|
| **Website URL:** | |
| **Username:** | |
| **Email:** | |
| **Password(s):** | |
| | |
| | |
| **Security Question/Notes** | |
| | |
| | |

| **I** |
|---|
| **Website URL:** |
| **Username:** |
| **Email:** |
| **Password(s):** |
| |
| |
| **Security Question/Notes** |
| |
| |

| **I** |
|---|
| **Website URL:** |
| **Username:** |
| **Email:** |
| **Password(s):** |
| |
| |
| **Security Question/Notes** |
| |
| |

| **I** |
|---|
| **Website URL:** |
| **Username:** |
| **Email:** |
| **Password(s):** |
| |
| |
| **Security Question/Notes** |
| |
| |

**I**

| Website URL: |
| --- |
| Username: |
| Email: |
| Password(s): |
| |
| |
| **Security Question/Notes** |
| |
| |

**I**

| Website URL: |
| --- |
| Username: |
| Email: |
| Password(s): |
| |
| |
| **Security Question/Notes** |
| |
| |

**I**

| Website URL: |
| --- |
| Username: |
| Email: |
| Password(s): |
| |
| |
| **Security Question/Notes** |
| |
| |

| |
|---|
| **Website URL:** |
| **Username:** |
| **Email:** |
| **Password(s):** |
| |
| |
| **Security Question/Notes** |
| |
| |

| |
|---|
| **Website URL:** |
| **Username:** |
| **Email:** |
| **Password(s):** |
| |
| |
| **Security Question/Notes** |
| |
| |

| |
|---|
| **Website URL:** |
| **Username:** |
| **Email:** |
| **Password(s):** |
| |
| |
| **Security Question/Notes** |
| |
| |

| |
|---|
| **Website URL:** |
| **Username:** |
| **Email:** |
| **Password(s):** |
| |
| |
| **Security Question/Notes** |
| |
| |

| |
|---|
| **Website URL:** |
| **Username:** |
| **Email:** |
| **Password(s):** |
| |
| |
| **Security Question/Notes** |
| |
| |

| |
|---|
| **Website URL:** |
| **Username:** |
| **Email:** |
| **Password(s):** |
| |
| |
| **Security Question/Notes** |
| |
| |

**J**

| Website URL: |
|---|
| Username: |
| Email: |
| Password(s): |
| |
| |
| **Security Question/Notes** |
| |
| |

**J**

| Website URL: |
|---|
| Username: |
| Email: |
| Password(s): |
| |
| |
| **Security Question/Notes** |
| |
| |

**J**

| Website URL: |
|---|
| Username: |
| Email: |
| Password(s): |
| |
| |
| **Security Question/Notes** |
| |
| |

## J

**Website URL:**

**Username:**

**Email:**

**Password(s):**



**Security Question/Notes**



## J

**Website URL:**

**Username:**

**Email:**

**Password(s):**



**Security Question/Notes**



## J

**Website URL:**

**Username:**

**Email:**

**Password(s):**



**Security Question/Notes**

**J**

| Website URL: |
| --- |
| Username: |
| Email: |
| Password(s): |
| |
| |
| Security Question/Notes |
| |
| |

**J**

| Website URL: |
| --- |
| Username: |
| Email: |
| Password(s): |
| |
| |
| Security Question/Notes |
| |
| |

**J**

| Website URL: |
| --- |
| Username: |
| Email: |
| Password(s): |
| |
| |
| Security Question/Notes |
| |
| |

**J**

| Website URL: |
| --- |
| Username: |
| Email: |
| Password(s): |
| |
| |
| Security Question/Notes |
| |
| |

**J**

| Website URL: |
| --- |
| Username: |
| Email: |
| Password(s): |
| |
| |
| Security Question/Notes |
| |
| |

**J**

| Website URL: |
| --- |
| Username: |
| Email: |
| Password(s): |
| |
| |
| Security Question/Notes |
| |
| |

**K**

| Website URL: |
|---|
| Username: |
| Email: |
| Password(s): |
| |
| |
| **Security Question/Notes** |
| |
| |

**K**

| Website URL: |
|---|
| Username: |
| Email: |
| Password(s): |
| |
| |
| **Security Question/Notes** |
| |
| |

**K**

| Website URL: |
|---|
| Username: |
| Email: |
| Password(s): |
| |
| |
| **Security Question/Notes** |
| |
| |

**K**

| Website URL: |
| --- |
| Username: |
| Email: |
| Password(s): |
| |
| |
| Security Question/Notes |
| |
| |

**K**

| Website URL: |
| --- |
| Username: |
| Email: |
| Password(s): |
| |
| |
| Security Question/Notes |
| |
| |

**K**

| Website URL: |
| --- |
| Username: |
| Email: |
| Password(s): |
| |
| |
| Security Question/Notes |
| |
| |

## K

**Website URL:**

**Username:**

**Email:**

**Password(s):**

**Security Question/Notes**

## K

**Website URL:**

**Username:**

**Email:**

**Password(s):**

**Security Question/Notes**

## K

**Website URL:**

**Username:**

**Email:**

**Password(s):**

**Security Question/Notes**

**K**

| Website URL: |
| --- |
| Username: |
| Email: |
| Password(s): |
| |
| |
| Security Question/Notes |
| |
| |

**K**

| Website URL: |
| --- |
| Username: |
| Email: |
| Password(s): |
| |
| |
| Security Question/Notes |
| |
| |

**K**

| Website URL: |
| --- |
| Username: |
| Email: |
| Password(s): |
| |
| |
| Security Question/Notes |
| |
| |

**L**

| | |
|---|---|
| **Website URL:** | |
| **Username:** | |
| **Email:** | |
| **Password(s):** | |
| | |
| | |
| **Security Question/Notes** | |
| | |
| | |

**L**

| | |
|---|---|
| **Website URL:** | |
| **Username:** | |
| **Email:** | |
| **Password(s):** | |
| | |
| | |
| **Security Question/Notes** | |
| | |
| | |

**L**

| | |
|---|---|
| **Website URL:** | |
| **Username:** | |
| **Email:** | |
| **Password(s):** | |
| | |
| | |
| **Security Question/Notes** | |
| | |
| | |

**L**

| | |
|---|---|
| **Website URL:** | |
| **Username:** | |
| **Email:** | |
| **Password(s):** | |
| | |
| | |
| **Security Question/Notes** | |
| | |
| | |

**L**

| | |
|---|---|
| **Website URL:** | |
| **Username:** | |
| **Email:** | |
| **Password(s):** | |
| | |
| | |
| **Security Question/Notes** | |
| | |
| | |

**L**

| | |
|---|---|
| **Website URL:** | |
| **Username:** | |
| **Email:** | |
| **Password(s):** | |
| | |
| | |
| **Security Question/Notes** | |
| | |
| | |

## L

| | |
|---|---|
| **Website URL:** | |
| **Username:** | |
| **Email:** | |
| **Password(s):** | |
| | |
| | |
| **Security Question/Notes** | |
| | |
| | |

## L

| | |
|---|---|
| **Website URL:** | |
| **Username:** | |
| **Email:** | |
| **Password(s):** | |
| | |
| | |
| **Security Question/Notes** | |
| | |
| | |

## L

| | |
|---|---|
| **Website URL:** | |
| **Username:** | |
| **Email:** | |
| **Password(s):** | |
| | |
| | |
| **Security Question/Notes** | |
| | |
| | |

## L

| | |
|---|---|
| **Website URL:** | |
| **Username:** | |
| **Email:** | |
| **Password(s):** | |
| | |
| | |
| **Security Question/Notes** | |
| | |
| | |

## L

| | |
|---|---|
| **Website URL:** | |
| **Username:** | |
| **Email:** | |
| **Password(s):** | |
| | |
| | |
| **Security Question/Notes** | |
| | |
| | |

## L

| | |
|---|---|
| **Website URL:** | |
| **Username:** | |
| **Email:** | |
| **Password(s):** | |
| | |
| | |
| **Security Question/Notes** | |
| | |
| | |

## M

| Website URL: |
|---|
| Username: |
| Email: |
| Password(s): |
| |
| |
| **Security Question/Notes** |
| |
| |

## M

| Website URL: |
|---|
| Username: |
| Email: |
| Password(s): |
| |
| |
| **Security Question/Notes** |
| |
| |

## M

| Website URL: |
|---|
| Username: |
| Email: |
| Password(s): |
| |
| |
| **Security Question/Notes** |
| |
| |

## M

| | |
|---|---|
| **Website URL:** | |
| **Username:** | |
| **Email:** | |
| **Password(s):** | |
| | |
| | |
| **Security Question/Notes** | |
| | |
| | |

## M

| | |
|---|---|
| **Website URL:** | |
| **Username:** | |
| **Email:** | |
| **Password(s):** | |
| | |
| | |
| **Security Question/Notes** | |
| | |
| | |

## M

| | |
|---|---|
| **Website URL:** | |
| **Username:** | |
| **Email:** | |
| **Password(s):** | |
| | |
| | |
| **Security Question/Notes** | |
| | |
| | |

## M

**Website URL:**

**Username:**

**Email:**

**Password(s):**



**Security Question/Notes**



## M

**Website URL:**

**Username:**

**Email:**

**Password(s):**



**Security Question/Notes**



## M

**Website URL:**

**Username:**

**Email:**

**Password(s):**



**Security Question/Notes**

**M**

| Website URL: |
|---|
| Username: |
| Email: |
| Password(s): |
| |
| |
| **Security Question/Notes** |
| |
| |

**M**

| Website URL: |
|---|
| Username: |
| Email: |
| Password(s): |
| |
| |
| **Security Question/Notes** |
| |
| |

**M**

| Website URL: |
|---|
| Username: |
| Email: |
| Password(s): |
| |
| |
| **Security Question/Notes** |
| |
| |

**N**

| Website URL: |
|---|
| Username: |
| Email: |
| Password(s): |
| |
| |
| **Security Question/Notes** |
| |
| |

**N**

| Website URL: |
|---|
| Username: |
| Email: |
| Password(s): |
| |
| |
| **Security Question/Notes** |
| |
| |

**N**

| Website URL: |
|---|
| Username: |
| Email: |
| Password(s): |
| |
| |
| **Security Question/Notes** |
| |
| |

## N

| | |
|---|---|
| **Website URL:** | |
| **Username:** | |
| **Email:** | |
| **Password(s):** | |
| | |
| | |
| **Security Question/Notes** | |
| | |
| | |

## N

| | |
|---|---|
| **Website URL:** | |
| **Username:** | |
| **Email:** | |
| **Password(s):** | |
| | |
| | |
| **Security Question/Notes** | |
| | |
| | |

## N

| | |
|---|---|
| **Website URL:** | |
| **Username:** | |
| **Email:** | |
| **Password(s):** | |
| | |
| | |
| **Security Question/Notes** | |
| | |
| | |

**N**

Website URL:

Username:

Email:

Password(s):

Security Question/Notes

---

**N**

Website URL:

Username:

Email:

Password(s):

Security Question/Notes

---

**N**

Website URL:

Username:

Email:

Password(s):

Security Question/Notes

**N**

| Website URL: |
| --- |
| Username: |
| Email: |
| Password(s): |
| |
| |
| Security Question/Notes |
| |
| |

**N**

| Website URL: |
| --- |
| Username: |
| Email: |
| Password(s): |
| |
| |
| Security Question/Notes |
| |
| |

**N**

| Website URL: |
| --- |
| Username: |
| Email: |
| Password(s): |
| |
| |
| Security Question/Notes |
| |
| |

**O**

| Website URL: |
| --- |
| Username: |
| Email: |
| Password(s): |
| |
| |
| **Security Question/Notes** |
| |
| |

**O**

| Website URL: |
| --- |
| Username: |
| Email: |
| Password(s): |
| |
| |
| **Security Question/Notes** |
| |
| |

**O**

| Website URL: |
| --- |
| Username: |
| Email: |
| Password(s): |
| |
| |
| **Security Question/Notes** |
| |
| |

**O**

| Website URL: |
| --- |
| Username: |
| Email: |
| Password(s): |
| |
| |
| Security Question/Notes |
| |
| |

**O**

| Website URL: |
| --- |
| Username: |
| Email: |
| Password(s): |
| |
| |
| Security Question/Notes |
| |
| |

**O**

| Website URL: |
| --- |
| Username: |
| Email: |
| Password(s): |
| |
| |
| Security Question/Notes |
| |
| |

## O

**Website URL:**

**Username:**

**Email:**

**Password(s):**

**Security Question/Notes**

## O

**Website URL:**

**Username:**

**Email:**

**Password(s):**

**Security Question/Notes**

## O

**Website URL:**

**Username:**

**Email:**

**Password(s):**

**Security Question/Notes**

**O**

| Website URL: |
| Username: |
| Email: |
| Password(s): |
| |
| |
| Security Question/Notes |
| |
| |

**O**

| Website URL: |
| Username: |
| Email: |
| Password(s): |
| |
| |
| Security Question/Notes |
| |
| |

**O**

| Website URL: |
| Username: |
| Email: |
| Password(s): |
| |
| |
| Security Question/Notes |
| |
| |

**P**

| | |
|---|---|
| **Website URL:** | |
| **Username:** | |
| **Email:** | |
| **Password(s):** | |
| | |
| | |
| **Security Question/Notes** | |
| | |
| | |

**P**

| | |
|---|---|
| **Website URL:** | |
| **Username:** | |
| **Email:** | |
| **Password(s):** | |
| | |
| | |
| **Security Question/Notes** | |
| | |
| | |

**P**

| | |
|---|---|
| **Website URL:** | |
| **Username:** | |
| **Email:** | |
| **Password(s):** | |
| | |
| | |
| **Security Question/Notes** | |
| | |
| | |

**P**

| Website URL: |
| Username: |
| Email: |
| Password(s): |
| |
| |
| Security Question/Notes |
| |
| |

**P**

| Website URL: |
| Username: |
| Email: |
| Password(s): |
| |
| |
| Security Question/Notes |
| |
| |

**P**

| Website URL: |
| Username: |
| Email: |
| Password(s): |
| |
| |
| Security Question/Notes |
| |
| |

**P**

Website URL:

Username:

Email:

Password(s):



Security Question/Notes




**P**

Website URL:

Username:

Email:

Password(s):



Security Question/Notes




**P**

Website URL:

Username:

Email:

Password(s):



Security Question/Notes

**P**

| Website URL: |
| Username: |
| Email: |
| Password(s): |
| |
| |
| Security Question/Notes |
| |
| |

**P**

| Website URL: |
| Username: |
| Email: |
| Password(s): |
| |
| |
| Security Question/Notes |
| |
| |

**P**

| Website URL: |
| Username: |
| Email: |
| Password(s): |
| |
| |
| Security Question/Notes |
| |
| |

**Q**

| Website URL: |
| Username: |
| Email: |
| Password(s): |
| |
| |
| Security Question/Notes |
| |
| |

**Q**

| Website URL: |
| Username: |
| Email: |
| Password(s): |
| |
| |
| Security Question/Notes |
| |
| |

**Q**

| Website URL: |
| Username: |
| Email: |
| Password(s): |
| |
| |
| Security Question/Notes |
| |
| |

**Q**

| Website URL: | |
|---|---|
| Username: | |
| Email: | |
| Password(s): | |
| | |
| | |
| **Security Question/Notes** | |
| | |
| | |

**Q**

| Website URL: | |
|---|---|
| Username: | |
| Email: | |
| Password(s): | |
| | |
| | |
| **Security Question/Notes** | |
| | |
| | |

**Q**

| Website URL: | |
|---|---|
| Username: | |
| Email: | |
| Password(s): | |
| | |
| | |
| **Security Question/Notes** | |
| | |
| | |

## Q

**Website URL:**

**Username:**

**Email:**

**Password(s):**

**Security Question/Notes**

## Q

**Website URL:**

**Username:**

**Email:**

**Password(s):**

**Security Question/Notes**

## Q

**Website URL:**

**Username:**

**Email:**

**Password(s):**

**Security Question/Notes**

**Q**

| Website URL: |
| --- |
| Username: |
| Email: |
| Password(s): |
| |
| |
| Security Question/Notes |
| |
| |

**Q**

| Website URL: |
| --- |
| Username: |
| Email: |
| Password(s): |
| |
| |
| Security Question/Notes |
| |
| |

**Q**

| Website URL: |
| --- |
| Username: |
| Email: |
| Password(s): |
| |
| |
| Security Question/Notes |
| |
| |

**R**

| Website URL: | |
|---|---|
| Username: | |
| Email: | |
| Password(s): | |
| | |
| | |
| Security Question/Notes | |
| | |
| | |

**R**

| Website URL: | |
|---|---|
| Username: | |
| Email: | |
| Password(s): | |
| | |
| | |
| Security Question/Notes | |
| | |
| | |

**R**

| Website URL: | |
|---|---|
| Username: | |
| Email: | |
| Password(s): | |
| | |
| | |
| Security Question/Notes | |
| | |
| | |

## R

| | |
|---|---|
| **Website URL:** | |
| **Username:** | |
| **Email:** | |
| **Password(s):** | |
| | |
| | |
| **Security Question/Notes** | |
| | |
| | |

## R

| | |
|---|---|
| **Website URL:** | |
| **Username:** | |
| **Email:** | |
| **Password(s):** | |
| | |
| | |
| **Security Question/Notes** | |
| | |
| | |

## R

| | |
|---|---|
| **Website URL:** | |
| **Username:** | |
| **Email:** | |
| **Password(s):** | |
| | |
| | |
| **Security Question/Notes** | |
| | |
| | |

**R**

| Website URL: |
| Username: |
| Email: |
| Password(s): |
| |
| |
| Security Question/Notes |
| |
| |

**R**

| Website URL: |
| Username: |
| Email: |
| Password(s): |
| |
| |
| Security Question/Notes |
| |
| |

**R**

| Website URL: |
| Username: |
| Email: |
| Password(s): |
| |
| |
| Security Question/Notes |
| |
| |

## R

| Website URL: |
| --- |
| Username: |
| Email: |
| Password(s): |
| |
| |
| Security Question/Notes |
| |
| |

## R

| Website URL: |
| --- |
| Username: |
| Email: |
| Password(s): |
| |
| |
| Security Question/Notes |
| |
| |

## R

| Website URL: |
| --- |
| Username: |
| Email: |
| Password(s): |
| |
| |
| Security Question/Notes |
| |
| |

## S

| | |
|---|---|
| **Website URL:** | |
| **Username:** | |
| **Email:** | |
| **Password(s):** | |
| | |
| | |
| **Security Question/Notes** | |
| | |
| | |

## S

| | |
|---|---|
| **Website URL:** | |
| **Username:** | |
| **Email:** | |
| **Password(s):** | |
| | |
| | |
| **Security Question/Notes** | |
| | |
| | |

## S

| | |
|---|---|
| **Website URL:** | |
| **Username:** | |
| **Email:** | |
| **Password(s):** | |
| | |
| | |
| **Security Question/Notes** | |
| | |
| | |

**S**

| Website URL: |
|---|
| Username: |
| Email: |
| Password(s): |
| |
| |
| Security Question/Notes |
| |
| |

**S**

| Website URL: |
|---|
| Username: |
| Email: |
| Password(s): |
| |
| |
| Security Question/Notes |
| |
| |

**S**

| Website URL: |
|---|
| Username: |
| Email: |
| Password(s): |
| |
| |
| Security Question/Notes |
| |
| |

## S

**Website URL:**

**Username:**

**Email:**

**Password(s):**

**Security Question/Notes**


## S

**Website URL:**

**Username:**

**Email:**

**Password(s):**

**Security Question/Notes**


## S

**Website URL:**

**Username:**

**Email:**

**Password(s):**

**Security Question/Notes**

**S**

| Website URL: |
| Username: |
| Email: |
| Password(s): |
| |
| |
| Security Question/Notes |
| |
| |

**S**

| Website URL: |
| Username: |
| Email: |
| Password(s): |
| |
| |
| Security Question/Notes |
| |
| |

**S**

| Website URL: |
| Username: |
| Email: |
| Password(s): |
| |
| |
| Security Question/Notes |
| |
| |

**T**

**Website URL:**

**Username:**

**Email:**

**Password(s):**



**Security Question/Notes**



---

**T**

**Website URL:**

**Username:**

**Email:**

**Password(s):**



**Security Question/Notes**



---

**T**

**Website URL:**

**Username:**

**Email:**

**Password(s):**



**Security Question/Notes**

**T**

| Website URL: |
| --- |
| Username: |
| Email: |
| Password(s): |
| |
| |
| Security Question/Notes |
| |
| |

**T**

| Website URL: |
| --- |
| Username: |
| Email: |
| Password(s): |
| |
| |
| Security Question/Notes |
| |
| |

**T**

| Website URL: |
| --- |
| Username: |
| Email: |
| Password(s): |
| |
| |
| Security Question/Notes |
| |
| |

**T**

| Website URL: |
| Username: |
| Email: |
| Password(s): |
| |
| |
| **Security Question/Notes** |
| |
| |

**T**

| Website URL: |
| Username: |
| Email: |
| Password(s): |
| |
| |
| **Security Question/Notes** |
| |
| |

**T**

| Website URL: |
| Username: |
| Email: |
| Password(s): |
| |
| |
| **Security Question/Notes** |
| |
| |

**T**

| Website URL: |
| --- |
| Username: |
| Email: |
| Password(s): |
| |
| |
| Security Question/Notes |
| |
| |

**T**

| Website URL: |
| --- |
| Username: |
| Email: |
| Password(s): |
| |
| |
| Security Question/Notes |
| |
| |

**T**

| Website URL: |
| --- |
| Username: |
| Email: |
| Password(s): |
| |
| |
| Security Question/Notes |
| |
| |

## U

| | |
|---|---|
| **Website URL:** | |
| **Username:** | |
| **Email:** | |
| **Password(s):** | |
| | |
| | |
| **Security Question/Notes** | |
| | |
| | |

## U

| | |
|---|---|
| **Website URL:** | |
| **Username:** | |
| **Email:** | |
| **Password(s):** | |
| | |
| | |
| **Security Question/Notes** | |
| | |
| | |

## U

| | |
|---|---|
| **Website URL:** | |
| **Username:** | |
| **Email:** | |
| **Password(s):** | |
| | |
| | |
| **Security Question/Notes** | |
| | |
| | |

## U

| | |
|---|---|
| **Website URL:** | |
| **Username:** | |
| **Email:** | |
| **Password(s):** | |
| | |
| | |
| **Security Question/Notes** | |
| | |
| | |

## U

| | |
|---|---|
| **Website URL:** | |
| **Username:** | |
| **Email:** | |
| **Password(s):** | |
| | |
| | |
| **Security Question/Notes** | |
| | |
| | |

## U

| | |
|---|---|
| **Website URL:** | |
| **Username:** | |
| **Email:** | |
| **Password(s):** | |
| | |
| | |
| **Security Question/Notes** | |
| | |
| | |

**U**

| Website URL: |
| --- |
| Username: |
| Email: |
| Password(s): |
| |
| |
| **Security Question/Notes** |
| |
| |

**U**

| Website URL: |
| --- |
| Username: |
| Email: |
| Password(s): |
| |
| |
| **Security Question/Notes** |
| |
| |

**U**

| Website URL: |
| --- |
| Username: |
| Email: |
| Password(s): |
| |
| |
| **Security Question/Notes** |
| |
| |

**U**

| | |
|---|---|
| **Website URL:** | |
| **Username:** | |
| **Email:** | |
| **Password(s):** | |
| | |
| | |
| **Security Question/Notes** | |
| | |
| | |

**U**

| | |
|---|---|
| **Website URL:** | |
| **Username:** | |
| **Email:** | |
| **Password(s):** | |
| | |
| | |
| **Security Question/Notes** | |
| | |
| | |

**U**

| | |
|---|---|
| **Website URL:** | |
| **Username:** | |
| **Email:** | |
| **Password(s):** | |
| | |
| | |
| **Security Question/Notes** | |
| | |
| | |

**V**

| Website URL: |
|---|
| Username: |
| Email: |
| Password(s): |
| |
| |
| **Security Question/Notes** |
| |
| |

**V**

| Website URL: |
|---|
| Username: |
| Email: |
| Password(s): |
| |
| |
| **Security Question/Notes** |
| |
| |

**V**

| Website URL: |
|---|
| Username: |
| Email: |
| Password(s): |
| |
| |
| **Security Question/Notes** |
| |
| |

## V

| | |
|---|---|
| **Website URL:** | |
| **Username:** | |
| **Email:** | |
| **Password(s):** | |
| | |
| | |
| **Security Question/Notes** | |
| | |
| | |

## V

| | |
|---|---|
| **Website URL:** | |
| **Username:** | |
| **Email:** | |
| **Password(s):** | |
| | |
| | |
| **Security Question/Notes** | |
| | |
| | |

## V

| | |
|---|---|
| **Website URL:** | |
| **Username:** | |
| **Email:** | |
| **Password(s):** | |
| | |
| | |
| **Security Question/Notes** | |
| | |
| | |

**V**

| Website URL: |
| Username: |
| Email: |
| Password(s): |
| |
| |
| **Security Question/Notes** |
| |
| |

**V**

| Website URL: |
| Username: |
| Email: |
| Password(s): |
| |
| |
| **Security Question/Notes** |
| |
| |

**V**

| Website URL: |
| Username: |
| Email: |
| Password(s): |
| |
| |
| **Security Question/Notes** |
| |
| |

**V**

**Website URL:**

**Username:**

**Email:**

**Password(s):**



**Security Question/Notes**



---

**V**

**Website URL:**

**Username:**

**Email:**

**Password(s):**



**Security Question/Notes**



---

**V**

**Website URL:**

**Username:**

**Email:**

**Password(s):**



**Security Question/Notes**

**W**

| Website URL: |
|---|
| Username: |
| Email: |
| Password(s): |
| |
| |
| Security Question/Notes |
| |
| |

**W**

| Website URL: |
|---|
| Username: |
| Email: |
| Password(s): |
| |
| |
| Security Question/Notes |
| |
| |

**W**

| Website URL: |
|---|
| Username: |
| Email: |
| Password(s): |
| |
| |
| Security Question/Notes |
| |
| |

**W**

Website URL:

Username:

Email:

Password(s):



Security Question/Notes



---

**W**

Website URL:

Username:

Email:

Password(s):



Security Question/Notes



---

**W**

Website URL:

Username:

Email:

Password(s):



Security Question/Notes

**W**

| Website URL: | |
|---|---|
| Username: | |
| Email: | |
| Password(s): | |
| | |
| | |
| Security Question/Notes | |
| | |
| | |

**W**

| Website URL: | |
|---|---|
| Username: | |
| Email: | |
| Password(s): | |
| | |
| | |
| Security Question/Notes | |
| | |
| | |

**W**

| Website URL: | |
|---|---|
| Username: | |
| Email: | |
| Password(s): | |
| | |
| | |
| Security Question/Notes | |
| | |
| | |

**W**

| Website URL: |
| --- |
| Username: |
| Email: |
| Password(s): |
| |
| |
| Security Question/Notes |
| |
| |

**W**

| Website URL: |
| --- |
| Username: |
| Email: |
| Password(s): |
| |
| |
| Security Question/Notes |
| |
| |

**W**

| Website URL: |
| --- |
| Username: |
| Email: |
| Password(s): |
| |
| |
| Security Question/Notes |
| |
| |

**X**

| | |
|---|---|
| **Website URL:** | |
| **Username:** | |
| **Email:** | |
| **Password(s):** | |
| | |
| | |
| **Security Question/Notes** | |
| | |
| | |

**X**

| | |
|---|---|
| **Website URL:** | |
| **Username:** | |
| **Email:** | |
| **Password(s):** | |
| | |
| | |
| **Security Question/Notes** | |
| | |
| | |

**X**

| | |
|---|---|
| **Website URL:** | |
| **Username:** | |
| **Email:** | |
| **Password(s):** | |
| | |
| | |
| **Security Question/Notes** | |
| | |
| | |

**X**

| Website URL: |
| --- |
| Username: |
| Email: |
| Password(s): |
| |
| |
| Security Question/Notes |
| |
| |

**X**

| Website URL: |
| --- |
| Username: |
| Email: |
| Password(s): |
| |
| |
| Security Question/Notes |
| |
| |

**X**

| Website URL: |
| --- |
| Username: |
| Email: |
| Password(s): |
| |
| |
| Security Question/Notes |
| |
| |

**X**

| Website URL: |
| Username: |
| Email: |
| Password(s): |
| |
| |
| **Security Question/Notes** |
| |
| |

**X**

| Website URL: |
| Username: |
| Email: |
| Password(s): |
| |
| |
| **Security Question/Notes** |
| |
| |

**X**

| Website URL: |
| Username: |
| Email: |
| Password(s): |
| |
| |
| **Security Question/Notes** |
| |
| |

**X**

| Website URL: |
| Username: |
| Email: |
| Password(s): |
| |
| |
| Security Question/Notes |
| |
| |

**X**

| Website URL: |
| Username: |
| Email: |
| Password(s): |
| |
| |
| Security Question/Notes |
| |
| |

**X**

| Website URL: |
| Username: |
| Email: |
| Password(s): |
| |
| |
| Security Question/Notes |
| |
| |

**Y**

| Website URL: |
| --- |
| Username: |
| Email: |
| Password(s): |
| |
| |
| Security Question/Notes |
| |
| |

**Y**

| Website URL: |
| --- |
| Username: |
| Email: |
| Password(s): |
| |
| |
| Security Question/Notes |
| |
| |

**Y**

| Website URL: |
| --- |
| Username: |
| Email: |
| Password(s): |
| |
| |
| Security Question/Notes |
| |
| |

**Y**

| Website URL: | |
|---|---|
| Username: | |
| Email: | |
| Password(s): | |
| | |
| | |
| Security Question/Notes | |
| | |
| | |

**Y**

| Website URL: | |
|---|---|
| Username: | |
| Email: | |
| Password(s): | |
| | |
| | |
| Security Question/Notes | |
| | |
| | |

**Y**

| Website URL: | |
|---|---|
| Username: | |
| Email: | |
| Password(s): | |
| | |
| | |
| Security Question/Notes | |
| | |
| | |

**Y**

| Website URL: |
| --- |
| Username: |
| Email: |
| Password(s): |
| |
| |
| **Security Question/Notes** |
| |
| |

**Y**

| Website URL: |
| --- |
| Username: |
| Email: |
| Password(s): |
| |
| |
| **Security Question/Notes** |
| |
| |

**Y**

| Website URL: |
| --- |
| Username: |
| Email: |
| Password(s): |
| |
| |
| **Security Question/Notes** |
| |
| |

## Y

| | |
|---|---|
| **Website URL:** | |
| **Username:** | |
| **Email:** | |
| **Password(s):** | |
| | |
| | |
| **Security Question/Notes** | |
| | |
| | |

## Y

| | |
|---|---|
| **Website URL:** | |
| **Username:** | |
| **Email:** | |
| **Password(s):** | |
| | |
| | |
| **Security Question/Notes** | |
| | |
| | |

## Y

| | |
|---|---|
| **Website URL:** | |
| **Username:** | |
| **Email:** | |
| **Password(s):** | |
| | |
| | |
| **Security Question/Notes** | |
| | |
| | |

**Z**

Website URL:

Username:

Email:

Password(s):



Security Question/Notes



---

**Z**

Website URL:

Username:

Email:

Password(s):



Security Question/Notes



---

**Z**

Website URL:

Username:

Email:

Password(s):



Security Question/Notes

**Z**

| Website URL: |
| Username: |
| Email: |
| Password(s): |
| |
| |
| Security Question/Notes |
| |
| |

**Z**

| Website URL: |
| Username: |
| Email: |
| Password(s): |
| |
| |
| Security Question/Notes |
| |
| |

**Z**

| Website URL: |
| Username: |
| Email: |
| Password(s): |
| |
| |
| Security Question/Notes |
| |
| |

## Z

**Website URL:**

**Username:**

**Email:**

**Password(s):**



**Security Question/Notes**



## Z

**Website URL:**

**Username:**

**Email:**

**Password(s):**



**Security Question/Notes**



## Z

**Website URL:**

**Username:**

**Email:**

**Password(s):**



**Security Question/Notes**

**Z**

| Website URL: |
| --- |
| Username: |
| Email: |
| Password(s): |
| |
| |
| Security Question/Notes |
| |
| |

**Z**

| Website URL: |
| --- |
| Username: |
| Email: |
| Password(s): |
| |
| |
| Security Question/Notes |
| |
| |

**Z**

| Website URL: |
| --- |
| Username: |
| Email: |
| Password(s): |
| |
| |
| Security Question/Notes |
| |
| |

www.ingramcontent.com/pod-product-compliance
Lightning Source LLC
LaVergne TN
LVHW080118070326
832902LV00015B/2652

* 9 7 8 1 5 3 2 8 0 2 9 2 8 *